REAL-LIFE MYSTERIES

CAN YOU EXPLAIN THE UNEXPLAINED?

| Written by | Susan Martineau |
| Designed & illustrated by | Vicky Barker |

www.bsmall.co.uk

Published by b small publishing ltd. www.bsmall.co.uk © b small publishing ltd. 2017 • 1 2 3 4 5 • ISBN 978-1-911509-08-0 •
Production by Madeleine Ehm.   Printed in China by WKT Co. Ltd.

CASE FILE
Real-life Mysteries

Everyone loves a good mystery. Here are some of the most intriguing cases of all time. Many people have tried to explain the truth behind them, but these mysteries are not so easily solved.

Read the amazing stories first. Then look at the CASE FILE for each one so that you can examine the evidence so far. Perhaps YOU will be the one to uncover the truth?

INVESTIGATING THE UNEXPLAINED...

Keep an open mind and your wits about you. Try to look carefully and objectively at the facts. It is easy to get carried away imagining all sorts of things that might hide the truth.

The aim of any investigation is to get proper evidence.

Objectively means looking at facts to make up your mind and not being influenced by emotions or fear!

WITNESSES

Interview people who say they have had an unusual or spooky experience. You could record what they say and write it up afterwards.

LOCATIONS

If you visit a place where mysterious things have happened make sure you do not go alone and always ask permission from a grown-up.

INVESTIGATOR'S KIT

Always keep a notebook and pen with you so that you can keep careful notes and draw diagrams if necessary.

Mystery Word

There is a complete list of the mystery words used in the book on the final page.

EVIDENCE

Prepare your facts and findings so that you can present them to your friends and family. They will be fascinated.

inexplicable

pseudoscience

FURTHER INVESTIGATIONS

These are suggested in some of the CASE FILES.
Over to you!

Scary, Hairy Creatures!

In 1967 two ranchers, Roger Patterson and Bob Gimlin, were riding through Bluff Creek in California. They saw a large, ape-like creature crouching by the river. As they rode towards it the huge beast stood up on its hind legs and the men could see it was covered in dark fur. As it strode away into the trees Patterson managed to film it, despite being thrown to the ground by his terrified horse. This was not the first time such a creature had been seen in the vast forests of North America. Even people who were used to being out there in the big woods had been totally spooked by the scary man-ape called BIGFOOT or SASQUATCH.

The name Sasquatch comes from a Native American word meaning 'wild man'. Each tribe had its own name for this gigantic creature.

Hunters and trappers in the 1800s told tales of massive footprints that looked oddly human. There were sightings of immensely tall creatures, covered in dark hair, with very long arms and small heads, no neck and huge shoulders.

Monster Word

cryptozoology

is the study of animals that remain hidden (cryptids). They may or may not exist!

More blood curdling still were stories of people being kidnapped or attacked by groups of Sasquatch. Country folk living in remote log cabins reported being terrorised by something unspeakable prowling outside. They would hear yowling and bizarre whistling noises unlike any other animal they had ever heard. It also had a foul smell!

The stories of sightings have never really stopped to this day. Many people in the northern areas of America and Canada have come forward to tell of their own encounters with Bigfoot in forests, in their backyards, or along remote country roads. Can they all be mistaken, or lying? What is BIGFOOT?

Turn over to read the **case file** notes...

CASE FILE - Bigfoot
The evidence so far...

Turn back to read the stories behind the case file...

Bluff Creek Video

The film taken in 1967 by Roger Patterson shows the creature turning to look at him and walking rapidly into the woods.

- Is it just someone in a gorilla suit?

- The Disney film company said at the time that it would have been very difficult and expensive to fake this and the movements of the animal.

Photos

A large number of these exist. Most of them are pretty blurry, but the people who took them were shocked and scared.

No bones or bodies have ever been found!

Giant Footsteps

Many Sasquatch footprints have been seen over the years and plaster casts have been taken of some of them.

- It is easy to fake these and some people have even admitted to making enormous wooden feet to produce joke prints.

- But some Bigfoot tracks are so detailed that 'fingerprints' (or dermatoglyphs) can be seen and these are very hard to fake.

Witness Statements

There is a long history of sightings. Does this make it more likely that there is some truth in them?

'My first impression was of a huge man, about six feet tall, almost three feet wide... covered from head to foot with dark brown silver-tipped hair.'

William Roe, Highway Worker, 1955.

'I am not entirely sure what I saw that day but I know it was not a bear and it was not a human.'

14-year-old boy out hunting, 1990.

Newspapers and the internet mean that Bigfoot stories can be spread all round the world. Maybe some people might make up a sighting to have their moment of fame?

Bigfoot Identikit

Height:
1.8-3 metres (6-10 feet).

Shoulders:
91 cm (3 feet) wide.

Fur:
dark brown or reddish brown, none around mouth and eyes.

Head:
conical, with ears on side.

Feet:
30-55 cm (1-1.8 feet) long.

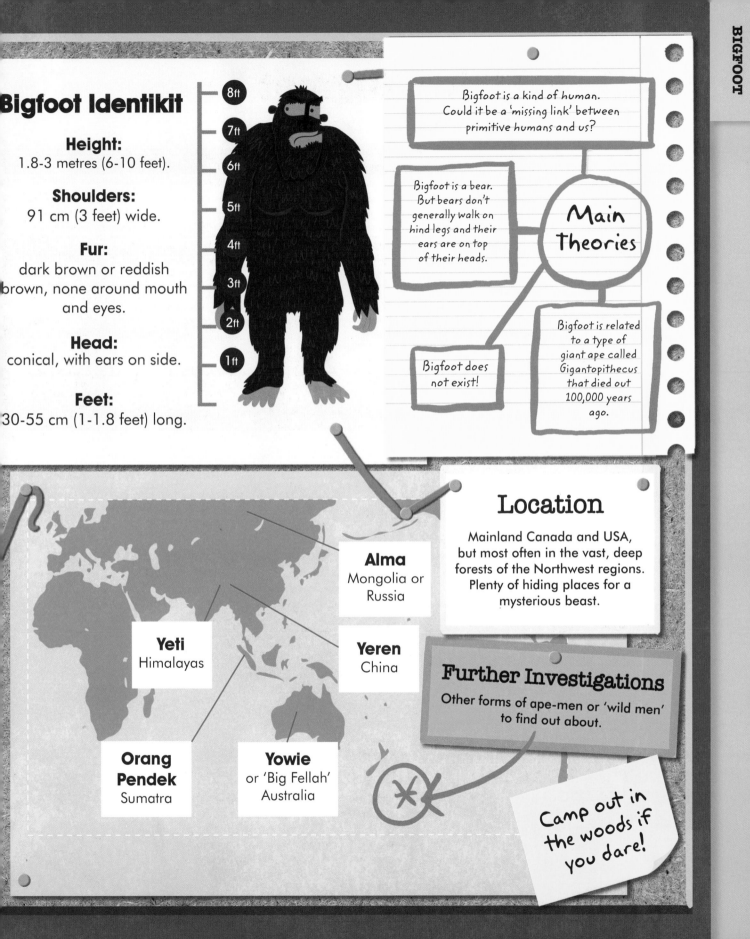

8ft
7ft
6ft
5ft
4ft
3ft
2ft
1ft

Bigfoot is a kind of human. Could it be a 'missing link' between primitive humans and us?

Bigfoot is a bear. But bears don't generally walk on hind legs and their ears are on top of their heads.

Main Theories

Bigfoot does not exist!

Bigfoot is related to a type of giant ape called Gigantopithecus that died out 100,000 years ago.

Alma
Mongolia or Russia

Yeti
Himalayas

Yeren
China

Orang Pendek
Sumatra

Yowie
or 'Big Fellah'
Australia

Location

Mainland Canada and USA, but most often in the vast, deep forests of the Northwest regions. Plenty of hiding places for a mysterious beast.

Further Investigations

Other forms of ape-men or 'wild men' to find out about.

Camp out in the woods if you dare!

Slipping into the Past

On a hot August day in 1901 two English women were visiting the palace of Versailles near Paris. Charlotte Moberly and Eleanor Jourdain were walking in the palace grounds near a smaller chateau called the Petit Trianon.

Charlotte and Eleanor had lost their way when they started to notice that all the other people in the gardens were dressed in old-fashioned costumes. The atmosphere felt flat and heavy. They saw two men in strange uniforms...

...and Charlotte also noticed there was a woman in a beautiful dress sitting sketching amongst the trees. When they returned from their walk they were astonished to learn that no one else had seen anyone dressed in an old style or a lady drawing that day.

They began to suspect that they had somehow seen a scene from the past. When they returned to the gardens they saw many new details and curious features, but they could not find a small bridge they had crossed the first time.

Charlotte and Eleanor were so intrigued by their experience that they published a book about what they had seen. They concluded that they had witnessed a version of the palace and gardens dating from the late 1700s. They thought that the lady sketching must be none other than the doomed queen of France, Marie Antoinette, who was executed in 1793.

Other people also claim to have observed strange things in the Versailles gardens and to have felt an unpleasant heaviness and gloom. There have also been more reports of a 'sketching lady' near the Petit Trianon and sightings of people dressed in the fashions of the eighteenth century.

Were they all just imagining things or could it be that they had experienced a view into the past?

Spooky Word

apparition

means the strange and unexpected appearance of someone or something.

Turn over to read the **case file** notes...

CASE FILE - Versailles
The evidence so far...

Turn back to read the story behind the case file...

Charlotte Moberly

Eleanor Jourdain

Location

The Petit Trianon and its gardens were where the eighteenth-century French queen, Marie Antoinette, used to get away from the main court of the palace of Versailles.

The gardens are full of winding paths, curious buildings and mysterious little glades. It is easy to get lost here!

The Evidence

There are no photos or any film footage of this incident. The evidence is in the form of witness statements by Moberly and Jourdain.

Petit Trianon

Witness Statements

Moberly and Jourdain's book about their experience was called An Adventure. It was published in 1911, ten years after their trip to Versailles. The women did not use their real names as the authors.

In 1958 a researcher called Guy Lambert said that the two women had indeed described the Petit Trianon as it would have appeared around 1770.

Witness Reliability

Charlotte Moberly was the principal of a college at Oxford University and Eleanor Jourdain was a headmistress. They would seem to be honest witnesses, but let's consider:

- Might they have seen old pictures of how the Petit Trianon and the gardens looked in the 18th century before their visit?

- Why did they wait so many years before publishing their book?

- Why did they not use their real names as the authors when the book was first published?

Main theories

The women experienced what is called a time-slip which meant they could 'tune into' the past. Perhaps time-slips are more likely in places where important historical events have happened?

The people in old-fashioned dress were at a fancy-dress party or historical reconstruction in the gardens. In this case their costumes were extremely accurate. The men in uniform looked exactly like the Swiss Guards who protected Marie Antoinette.

A mysterious place, like these gardens, might lead you to imagine something intriguing. Then the more you tell the story the more you believe you've seen something strange!

Further Investigations

Some ghost stories describe the apparition 'floating' along the ground. Is this a 'time-slip'? The ground might have been higher and less worn-down in the past.

Tell your friends an interesting story. Then ask them to tell it back to you a week later. See if it's the same story!

Unidentified Flying Objects

In 1947 a pilot called Kenneth Arnold was flying over Mount Rainier in Washington, USA when he saw some strange crescent-shaped aircraft moving at huge speed.

Arnold described the objects as flying like a saucer would if you skimmed it across the water. Newspaper reports then called them 'flying saucers', and this name has been used to describe many UFOs (Unidentified Flying Objects) ever since.

During the 1970s many people reported seeing large triangular aircraft moving slowing and silently across the sky. These mysterious objects were seen mainly across the skies of England and Europe. They did not look like any aircraft ever seen before.

In 1974 people in Llandrillo, Wales were frightened by a massive explosion and rumbling sound. They could also see bright lights moving quickly across the night sky. Army officials soon appeared on the scene and stories spread that a UFO had crashed on a nearby mountain. It was rumoured that its alien passengers had been taken away in secrecy by the army.

In 1978 in New Zealand strange lights were spotted in the skies off the coast of Kaikoura. Air traffic controllers could not identify them as any known aircraft. Many anxious people called the local police as they could see powerful beams of light being projected on to the sea from the craft.

Cargo plane spots strange lights.

These are just a very few of the thousands of stories told about UFOs. What are these objects and where do they come from?

Unidentified Weird Lights

Hessdalen Lights

Yellowish, bullet-shaped lights and small red dots were seen in the sky in a remote region of Norway in the 1980s. Investigators flashed a laser beam at one light and it seemed to send answering flashes.

Sea Lights

For centuries sailors have reported seeing swirling wheels of light below the surface of the sea in the Persian Gulf and Indian Ocean. The wheels sometimes appear to rise spookily above the water.

Foo Fighters

Mysterious balls of light were seen in the skies by World War Two fighter pilots in the 1940s. These unidentifiable lights would fly near to or alongside their aircraft.

Turn over to read the **case file** notes...

CASE FILE - UFOs
The evidence so far...

Turn back to read the stories behind the case file...

WITNESSES
Thousands of people all over the world.

Key Witness

Kenneth Arnold, a pilot, who first described UFOs as 'flying like a saucer'.
He became the world's first private UFO investigator. He interviewed many other people who claimed to have seen strange flying objects in the sky.

An FBI officer interviewed Kenneth Arnold and stated: *'It is the personal opinion of the interviewer that he actually saw what he states he saw.'*

Time

Modern sightings began with Kenneth Arnold in 1947. Many of the reports date from the era of humans' first space exploration. Perhaps people had spaceships on the brain!

Evidence

Many photos and films. These are easy to fake or take from an angle that makes something normal look weird.

The Kaikoura UFOs were captured on film by a journalist on board a cargo plane. You can hear the real fear in the voices of the witnesses on the soundtrack.

Description

Different shapes and forms. After the 'flying saucer' label was used many people said they had seen saucer-shaped UFOs.

Alien Word
ufology ↴

(you-follow-gee) is the study of unidentified flying objects (UFOs).

UFOs are really aircraft, weather balloons, satellites, or a trick of the light.

Arnold was seeing reflections on his aircraft canopy, missiles, snow flurries or birds in flight. Arnold totally disagreed with these suggestions.

Flying triangles were stealth bombers and test planes, but there has never been any official government explanation.

Over 20 different theories were suggested for the Kaikoura sightings, but it is still not known what those UFOs were doing there or where they had come from.

Main theories

Could the Llandrillo incident have been an earth tremor or hunters with powerful lights? But why did the army appear so quickly on the scene and warn people to stay away?

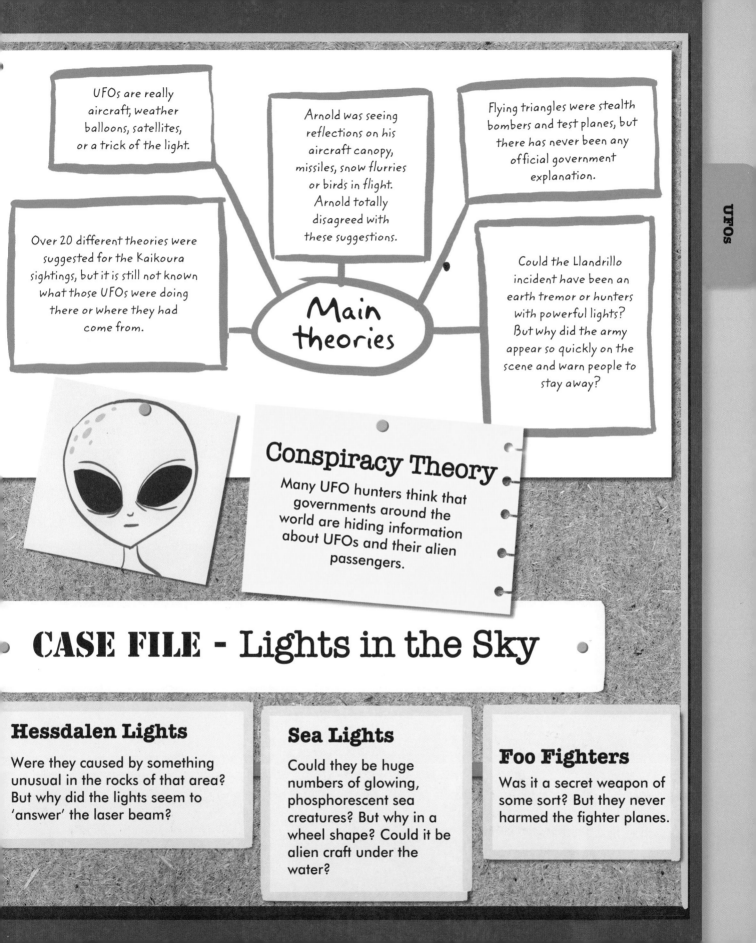

Conspiracy Theory

Many UFO hunters think that governments around the world are hiding information about UFOs and their alien passengers.

CASE FILE - Lights in the Sky

Hessdalen Lights

Were they caused by something unusual in the rocks of that area? But why did the lights seem to 'answer' the laser beam?

Sea Lights

Could they be huge numbers of glowing, phosphorescent sea creatures? But why in a wheel shape? Could it be alien craft under the water?

Foo Fighters

Was it a secret weapon of some sort? But they never harmed the fighter planes.

Ancient Alien Astronauts

Is it possible that space travellers from other planets visited Earth many thousands of years ago? And did those alien visitors share their knowledge of science and technology with the humans alive then?

Some people believe that there are places and objects left behind from that time and they call these visito ancient astronauts. In 1968 an author called Erich von Däniken published a book called *Chariots of the Gods?* in which he put forward this amazing idea.

Nazca Lines

In the high desert of Peru in South America there are hundreds of huge shapes on the ground. Some look like animals or humans, but there are also enormous long straight lines running for hundreds of metres. It looks like they are meant to be seen from above. Erich von Däniken suggested that they were runways and landing sites for alien spaceships.

Phaistos Disc

This mysterious disc is engraved with strange symbols in a spiral shape. The disc was found in Phaistos on the island of Crete. It seems to date from thousands of years ago during the time of the ancient Minoan civilization. No one has been able to decipher the symbols completely and some people say that this is because they are in an alien language.

The Great Pyramid

This is the largest of the pyramids of Egypt and one of the legendary Seven Wonders of the World. It was probably meant to be a tomb for Pharaoh Khufu (or Cheops). It was built using over two million massive limestone blocks. They fit together so precisely that a knife cannot be pushed between them. How on earth did people who lived so long ago manage to build such a wonder without space-age technology?

Stonehenge

A colossal circle of stones called Stonehenge stands on Salisbury Plain in southern England. The stones are so enormous that it would have been incredibly difficult to move them and put them into position at a time when the wheel had not even been invented. Could it be that Stonehenge is a model of our solar system and ancient astronauts helped to build it?

Turn over to read the **case file** notes...

CASE FILE - Alien Astronauts
The evidence so far...

Turn back to read the stories behind the case file...

Stonehenge

Location: England

Age: over 4,500 years.

Description: circle made of huge stones. Some come from Wales, 250 km (155 miles) away and each weighs between 2 and 5 tonnes.

This is how Stonehenge might have looked.

Phaistos Disc

Location: Crete

Age: possibly 4,000 years.

Description: clay disc about 16 cm (6 inches) in diameter. Covered in a spiral of stamped symbols on both sides. Some have been decoded but not all.

Nazca Lines

Location: Peru

Age: over 2,000 years.

Description: over 300 patterns including animals such as spiders, birds and monkeys. Long lines and abstract shapes.

The Great Pyramid

Location: Egypt

Age: about 4,700 years.

Description: biggest of all the pyramids. It is 146 metres (479 feet) high. Contains about 2.3 million blocks of stone. Each weighs 2 tonnes.

479 ft

Was this an alien building project? Were space travellers building some sort of observatory to watch the stars?

OR

Did prehistoric humans build it using the basic stone tools that archaeologists have discovered at the site? Was it a temple where people gathered to watch the movements of the sun?

Is it some kind of alien computer hard-drive? The Minoans were a highly advanced civilization. Did they get their knowledge from travellers from outer space?

BUT

Why would space travellers use a clay disc? It is not very hi-tech. Archaeologists think that the symbols are probably a Minoan prayer.

Are they landing sites used by visitors from outer space?

OR

Were they created by the Nazca people, who lived in Peru from about 200 BC to AD 500, as a religious site or even some kind of chart of the stars?

Witness Statements

Several books have been published about the idea of aliens visiting Earth long ago. Bestselling book by Erich von Däniken made this idea of ancient astronauts popular.

Von Däniken born 1935. Worked as hotel manager. Not a scientist or historian.

Just because something is written in a book does not mean it is true!

Did the Ancient Egyptians receive help from space travellers to build this amazing pyramid?

OR

Did they manage perfectly well with their own tools and techniques and thousands of workers?

Reconstruction

Archaeological experiments have succeeded in moving MEGALITHS (big stones) using the simple tools that would have been available at the time.

Mystery Word

pseudoscience

means theories about the world that are NOT based on science. 'Pseudo' means 'false' in Greek.

Curses, Curses, Curses!

Is it possible for something to be cursed or jinxed? Can a ship, a jewel or a car bring you bad luck?

The Haunted Ship

When the *SS Great Eastern* was launched in 1858 she was the largest ship in the world. The great British engineer Isambard Kingdom Brunel designed her. However, the ship seemed doomed from the start.

Two workmen disappeared during its construction. An accident during the launch killed another workman and Brunel himself fell seriously ill. Then came the dreadful news that a steam pipe had burst and killed six more men. Poor Brunel died.

The ship was broken up for scrap only 15 years after it was built. As they took it apart the workmen found a gruesome discovery: two skeletons sealed up in the hull.

The Jinxed Jewel

There is a mysterious treasure called the Hope Diamond in the Smithsonian Institute in Washington DC in America. It is named after one of its many owners.

The diamond is said to have been stolen in the seventeenth century from the eye socket of a temple statue in Myanmar. Since then, it seems to have brought bad luck to many of its owners, including Queen Marie Antoinette who was executed during the French Revolution in 1793.

Other victims have included a Russian prince who was murdered, a French jeweller who went mad and a Turkish sultan who killed his wife. The wealthy McLean family of America also suffered tragedy when they owned the jewel. However, the owner called Hope escaped unharmed!

The Cursed Car

James Dean was a young Hollywood actor. On 30th September 1955 he was driving his silver Porsche when he crashed into another car and was killed. He was only 24 years old.

Many of his friends had warned him about this car and said there was something sinister about it. Just a few days before the accident the actor Alec Guinness warned Dean: 'Get rid of that car, or you'll be dead in a week'.

After the accident the car caused more trouble. It rolled off the back of a truck and crushed the legs of a mechanic. Parts of the vehicle were reused in other cars and all of them were involved in dreadful accidents. While the chassis of the Porsche was being stored in a garage there was a terrible fire in the building. Weirdly, the car itself was unharmed.

Weird Word

supernatural

comes from the Latin for 'beyond nature'. It describes something that cannot be explained by what we know about the world around us.

Turn over to read the **case file** notes...

CASE FILE - Curses
The evidence so far...

Turn back to read the stories behind the case file...

The Great Eastern

The Victims

Several workmen.

Brunel himself.

Two workmen vanish and no bodies found until ship is broken up.

The Ship

The biggest steamship of her time.

Nearly 213 metres (700 feet) long and 25 metres (83 feet) wide.

Very expensive to build. The company that built her went bust.

Theories

Brunel was exhausted by hard work and this may have made him ill.

The missing workman were not found so their deaths jinxed the ship.

Building such a huge ship was very difficult so accidents were bound to happen.

The Hope Diamond

The Jewel

A blue Indian diamond about the size of a walnut.

It has had about 21 owners.

Under certain lights it shines with a blood-red glow.

Ultraviolet light causes this type of diamond to glow red.

The Victims

gone mad

died

committed murder

been murdered

had accidents

Some owners have been left unharmed.

Theories

James Dean's Car

The Victims

James Dean died in the crash.

His passenger survived, but died in another crash years later.

The Car

A silver Porsche 550 Spyder.

The car was designed for racing.

There was something spooky about the vehicle. After the accident it continued to cause trouble for some supernatural reason.

Theories

James Dean was driving much too fast. The police had already given him a speeding ticket earlier that day.

The parts of the car that were reused were damaged and should not have been used again.

The odd events that followed the accident were all just strange coincidences.

The Hindu priests of the temple put a curse on the diamond after it was stolen.

What happened to the victims would have happened anyway. A diamond cannot really have caused the French Revolution and the death of the French queen.

The story has been exaggerated, by newspapers and in books. Even Evalyn McLean liked to boast that she was wearing a cursed jewel!

Self-fulfilling Prophecy

This is an interesting theory that says if we think something is going to happen then we might behave in such a way that it actually does happen.

Helpful Ghosts

Spectral Sailor

There are many strange and fantastic stories about people in difficulty being helped by a ghostly presence. The famous nineteenth-century yachtsman, Joshua Slocum, experienced something most unusual on his solo voyage around the world.

As Slocum crossed the North Atlantic in 1895 a huge storm blew up and, to make matters worse, he fell ill with terrible stomach pains. Poor, half-fainting Slocum struggled to get back on deck to control his battered boat. As he reached the hatchway of his cabin he felt the boat steady herself and was amazed to see a man in fifteenth-century clothes at the helm.

The stranger introduced himself as helmsman of the *Pinta,* one of the ships used by Christopher Columbus to sail to America in 1492. He reassured Slocum that he would guide the boat while he slept. The boat and Slocum survived to tell the tale!

Chatty Phantoms

In May 1927 American aviator, Charles Lindbergh, was the first person to fly alone and non-stop from New York to Paris. It took him 33 hours. One of his greatest challenges was to stay awake. Afterwards he spoke of 'phantoms' on board his plane 'conversing and advising on my flight'.

The Invisible Companion

In 1916 the polar explorers Sir Ernest Shackleton, Frank Worsley and Tom Crean set off on a terrible trek across the icy mountains on the island of South Georgia, near Antarctica. They were trying to reach a whaling station on the other side of the island to fetch help for the rest of their expedition after their ship had been destroyed by ice.

At the time they did not speak to each other about the uncanny feeling they all had that there was a fourth silent companion on that difficult journey. It was only later that they all admitted that they had felt there was some invisible person there with them who helped them to keep going.

Spooky Space

In 1997 NASA astronaut, Jerry Linenger, spent five months on board the Russian space station MIR. There were many dangerous incidents during this mission, including a serious fire and near-collision with a supply ship. Jerry says he was aware of the presence of his dead father comforting him and telling him that everything would be all right.

Turn over to read the **case file** notes...

CASE FILE - Ghosts
The evidence so far...

Turn back to read the stories behind the case file...

Witnesses

Brave, adventurous and practical people who are used to pushing themselves to their limits.
They do not seem like people who would expect to have spooky experiences.

Locations

- High altitude in aircraft
- Space
- Extreme places
- Atlantic Ocean
- Antarctica
- Life or death situations

Witness Statements

Some of the witnesses wrote books about their adventures and mentioned these otherworldly experiences.

From *South* by Ernest Shackleton:

'...during that long and racking march of thirty-six hours over the unnamed mountains and glaciers of South Georgia, it seemed to me often that we were four, not three.'

SOUTH
SHACKLETON

From *Sailing Alone Around the World* by Joshua Slocum:

'...looking out of the companionway, to my amazement I saw a tall man at the helm.'

Sailing Alone Around the World

Captain Joshua Slocum

Main theories

Our brains can conjure up an extra 'person' as a way of helping us to cope with difficult times. It is a **survival mechanism** sometimes called **third man syndrome.** (Although in Shackleton's case it was a fourth man!)

Neuroscientists (brain scientists) have done experiments with people to see if they can make them feel as if another person is with them. They have done this by stimulating certain parts of the brain.

Does this mean our brains switch on a kind of 'autopilot' in times of stress and danger? We think we are hearing and feeling another person, but it is coming from within ourselves.

In times of danger and trouble helpful ghosts visit us. This is spooky, but rather comforting.

Slocum might have been delirious with fever and imagined it all.

Lindbergh was very tired and this could have made him imagine voices.

Ghostly Word

spectre

is another word for a ghost, phantom or apparition.

Monsters of the Deep

For as long as people have sailed the seas there have been tales of gigantic monsters or sea serpents that rear up out of the waves. Are we any closer to finding out what might be lurking down in the depths?

In 1848 *HMS Daedalus* was sailing in the South Atlantic Ocean when Captain Peter M'Quhae and six of his crew spotted an enormous creature swimming past the ship.

The mysterious beast was about 18 metres (60 feet) long with a large snake-like head that it held high above the waves. The monster was dark brown with a yellowish white throat and seemed to have a kind of shaggy mane along its back.

Sketch of the Brazil sea serpent drawn by a witness.

In 1905 two members of the British Royal Zoological Society reported another strange sighting off the coast of Brazil. They saw a large fin or frill sticking out of the water with a great big head and neck in front of it. They could also see the shape of an enormous body under the water.

San Francisco Bay in the USA also seems to have something mysterious living in the water. On 5th February 1985, brothers Bill and Bob Clark spotted an 18-metre (60-foot) long, snake-like beast chasing seals. It was moving its body up and down, making humps in the water. They could also see its yellowy underbelly and a fan-shaped fin.

The Legendary Kraken

The Kraken is the name given to a terrifying sea monster that makes an appearance in many traditional old tales of the sea. Is it possible that a Kraken exists in real life?

In March 1941 a group of British sailors was on a life raft in the South Atlantic Ocean. They were attacked by jellyfish and sharks, but worse was to come. An enormous creature rose up out of the depths, grabbed a sailor in its powerful tentacles and dragged him into the sea.

This scary monster and the Kraken of the stories might be some kind of gigantic squid. These deep-sea creatures do exist, although not much is known about them. They have huge grasping tentacles and arms equipped with suckers and hooks. They definitely sound like the sort of squid that would have you for dinner!

Turn over to read the **case file** notes...

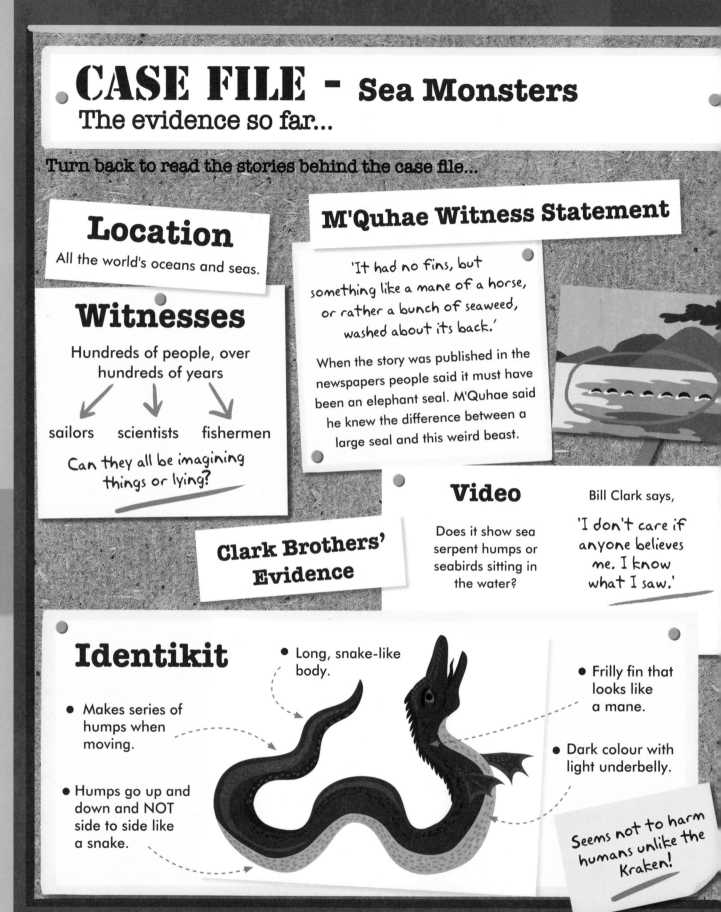

CASE FILE - Sea Monsters
The evidence so far...

Turn back to read the stories behind the case file...

Location

All the world's oceans and seas.

Witnesses

Hundreds of people, over hundreds of years

↙ ↓ ↘

sailors   scientists   fishermen

Can they all be imagining things or lying?

M'Quhae Witness Statement

'It had no fins, but something like a mane of a horse, or rather a bunch of seaweed, washed about its back.'

When the story was published in the newspapers people said it must have been an elephant seal. M'Quhae said he knew the difference between a large seal and this weird beast.

Video

Does it show sea serpent humps or seabirds sitting in the water?

Bill Clark says,

'I don't care if anyone believes me. I know what I saw.'

Clark Brothers' Evidence

Identikit

- Makes series of humps when moving.

- Humps go up and down and NOT side to side like a snake.

• Long, snake-like body.

• Frilly fin that looks like a mane.

• Dark colour with light underbelly.

Seems not to harm humans unlike the Kraken!

People are mistaking creatures like whales, eels, seals, sharks or oarfish for sea serpents. Oarfish can grow up to 11 metres (36 feet) long.

Oarfish

Sea serpents might be some sort of animal left over from the ancient past. Perhaps it is a marine dinosaur!

We only know a tiny fraction about life in the oceans so it is possible that there is an amazing beast like a sea serpent.

Main theories

The prehistoric **coelacanth** (SEEL-uh-kanth) was thought to have been extinct until a fisherman pulled one up from the depths in 1938.

Nessie's Cousins?

The famous Loch Ness Monster is said to lurk in the extremely deep Loch Ness in Scotland. Many people say they have sighted and even photographed the beast. Some believe it is possible that it is a type of dinosaur called a plesiosaur. Others say that all the photos and sightings are hoaxes.

Nessie may not be the only lake-lurking monster in the world!

Mokele Mbembe

Lives in the swamplands of the Congo in Africa.

Strange dinosaur-like creature that seems to be able to walk on land too.

Selma

Lives in Lake Seljordsvatnet, Norway.

A hump-backed, black creature with long body. Underwater sonar equipment has detected moving objects that may be 18 metres (60 feet) long.

Ogopogo

Lives in Lake Okanagan, Canada.

In 1974 a vast undulating creature in the water bumped into a swimmer.

Beastly Word
undulating

means moving like a wave, either up and down or side to side.

Fire from Within

John Irving Bentley was a retired doctor living in Pennsylvania, USA. He was last seen alive on 4th December 1966. The next morning a gasman called Don Gosnell let himself into Mr Bentley's house to read the meter in the basement. He had a key because Mr Bentley was very elderly and disabled.

Don Gosnell was surprised to see a pile of ash in the basement. As he went upstairs he noticed a light blue haze of smoke in the house and a sickly, sweet smell.

In the bathroom he was horrified to see the burnt remains of Mr Bentley. All that was left of him was a bit of right leg with the slipper still on the foot. Mr Bentley's walking frame was lying across a huge burnt hole in the floor, directly above the basement and the pile of ash. The rest of the room was strangely undamaged.

Poor Gosnell ran screaming out of the house shouting: 'Doctor Bentley's burned up!'

For centuries there have been stories of humans suddenly bursting into flames for no apparent reason. The name given to this mystery is Spontaneous Human Combustion or SHC. The victim's body, or most of it, is completely burnt up. A sticky pile of ash is left behind, but the surroundings are hardly damaged.

In 1725 a woman called Nicole Millet was found burnt to death in Reims, France. The chair she was sitting in was untouched by the fire. Madame Millet's husband was charged with murder. Luckily for him a doctor thought there was something odd about the case and managed to convince the court that she had been a victim of Spontaneous Human Combustion.

In 1731 an elderly Italian countess died in a sudden fire that did not damage the room she was in. All that was left of Countess Bandi were her legs and three fingers. The nineteenth-century English writer, Charles Dickens, was so intrigued by this story that he included a case of SHC in one of his novels, *Bleak House*.

BLEAK HOUSE

Cases of SHC are very rare but, as recently as 2010, an elderly man in Ireland died in such mysterious circumstances that investigators had to put it down to Spontaneous Human Combustion.

Turn over to read the **case file** notes...

CASE FILE - Spontaneous Human Combustion
The evidence so far...

Turn back to read the stories behind the case file...

Key Words

Spontaneous means something happens without any obvious cause.

Spontaneous human combustion is when a person bursts into flames and the cause cannot be found. The fire seems to come from within the body.

Witnesses

Usually no witnesses. Victims often on their own in a closed room. This makes it difficult for investigators to know EXACTLY what happened and what started the fire.

Clues

🔥 Photos of scenes usually show intense incineration of the victim. Nothing but an arm or leg is left.

🔥 The surrounding room and furnishings are often not very damaged.

🔥 In the Bentley case there was a hole burnt in the floor. The ash had fallen into the basement below in a neat pile. The fire had not spread.

🔥 In other cases sticky ash was found on furniture.

Victims
Most victims of SHC are elderly.

The Bentley Case - he was a smoker, but his pipe was found in his bedroom. Could he have dropped burning ash on himself, tried to get water from the bathroom, but fallen and knocked himself out? Maybe the flames then took hold and killed him.

The Wick Effect - the victims may already be unconscious, through illness or too much alcohol. They are too near to the source of a fire, like a cigarette or open fire. The body becomes like a human candle with the fat burning with a slow, but intense, heat. This is why the ashes are fatty. Don Gosnell described the smell in Bentley's house as:

'somewhat sweet, like starting up a new oil-burning central heating system.'

Freaky lightning called **ball lightning** strikes a person and does not touch anything else around them.

Main theories

There is some **unexplained electrical charge** within the body itself that causes it to burst into flames.

There must be some **scientific explanation** for the fire, but the bodies are so badly burnt that it is impossible to tell what caused it.

1 Unconscious victim

2 Fat burns in centre of body.

3 Body largely consumed by fire.

But why doesn't the fire spread to other parts of the room?

Fiery Word

incineration is when something is burnt to ashes.

Astonishing Superpowers

Walking On Fire

Every May there is a festival in northern Greece and southern Bulgaria. As part of the celebrations people walk barefoot across a layer of burning wood.

This is just one of many religious ceremonies around the world during which people walk across burning coals or wood without harming themselves.

The Hindu festival of Thimithi includes walking across a fire-pit.

On the Indonesian island of Bali young boys and girls perform a sacred dance called Sanghyang around and across a fire.

Bending Spoons

In the 1970s a man called Uri Geller became very famous for seeming to be able to bend spoons and other metal objects without using any force.

Audiences would watch him gently stroking a spoon and be amazed to see the handle bend.

Many other people claim that they can create similar paranormal effects, using the power of their minds.

Superpower Word

paranormal

means something that does not have an obvious scientific explanation.

Finding Water

Looking for water using a technique called dowsing has been done for thousands of years. Dowsing is also used to search for buried metals, oil and even missing people.

The searchers, or dowsers, use a special tool. This is often a forked wooden stick called a dowsing or divining rod. The dowser holds the forked end of the rod with one fork in each hand.

The dowser then walks around the search area until the end of the rod twitches and dips down. The more it moves the nearer the dowser is to what they are looking for.

Seeing the Future

Some people claim they have a 'sixth sense' that allows them to see into the future, often in their dreams. This mysterious ability is also called ESP or Extrasensory Perception.

President Abraham Lincoln of America is said to have had a dream in which he foresaw his own death. A few days later, on 14th April 1865, he was shot during a visit to the theatre. He died the next day.

After the tragic sinking of the ocean liner *Titanic* in 1912 many people said that they had had a premonition that there would be a disaster. Some even refused to sail in her at the last minute.

Turn over to read the **case file** notes...

CASE FILE – Superpowers

The evidence so far...

Turn back to read the stories behind the case file...

Fire-walking

Theories

* People can walk over fire and hot coals and wood because they are in a state of mind where they feel no pain.

* The feet do not conduct (or carry) heat very well so if you keep moving there is not much risk of getting burnt.

* The layer of ashes over the hot coals or wood helps to stop too much heat being transmitted into the feet.

You can snuff out a candle with a quick pinch of your fingers without it burning you.

DO NOT TRY THIS AT HOME!

NEVER PLAY WITH FIRE OR CANDLES.

Spoon-bending

Theories

* Some people can manipulate (bend or move) solid objects using only the power of their minds. Psychokinesis is the word used to describe this ability.

* It is a very clever trick or illusion practised by magicians.

If you hold a spoon by its neck and quickly tilt it backwards and forwards it can look as if the spoon is bending. You can see videos on the internet of how to do this.

Finding Water

Theories

* Dowsers have magical powers which make their rods or sticks twitch.

* Dowsers are tuning into a special force that makes their muscles twitch and the rod move.

* Dowsers are picking up clues in the environment that help them detect the most likely places to find what they are looking for.

Rhabdomancy

is another name for dowsing with rods.

Seeing the Future

Theories

* Some people would say **ESP** or **Extrasensory Perception** is a special ability to predict what will happen in the future, but scientists have not been able to prove it exists.

* Like many people in important positions Lincoln would have known he was in danger of assassination.

* The *Titanic* was the biggest liner ever built at that time and so people might well have felt nervous about how safe it was.

TITANIC SINKS!
MORE THAN 1500 DEAD.

LINCOLN SHOT
1809-1865

Superpower Word

premonition

is a strong feeling that something unpleasant or horrible is about to happen.

Superpower Word

parapsychology

is the study of mental abilities that cannot be explained by what scientists know about nature and the world.

Psychic Detectives

Psychometry is the name given to the ability to detect information about someone by touching objects that belong to them. Psychometrists say they can hold an object owned by a missing person to sense what has happened to them.

Strange Circles

Patterns in the Fields

In 2001 an amazing pattern appeared overnight in a field at Milk Hill in the county of Wiltshire in the UK. It was 266 metres (878 feet) across with 409 circles in a fantastic spiral. Who or what on earth had made it and why was it there?

This crop circle was one of many mysterious designs that have appeared in fields all over the world. The crop is not cut, but usually looks as if it has been carefully flattened to make all kinds of shapes and patterns.

These intriguing formations only appear during the growing season of the crops. Although they are found in many other countries, most of them occur in the UK in Wiltshire. They have even been seen very near to the ancient stone circle of Stonehenge.

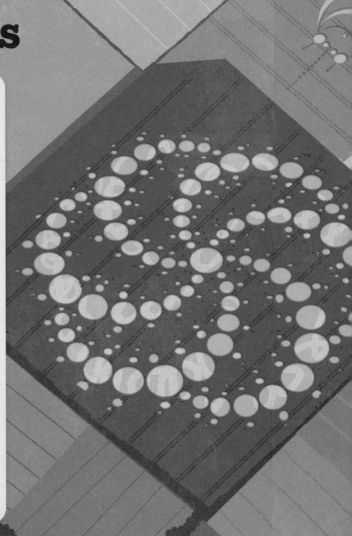

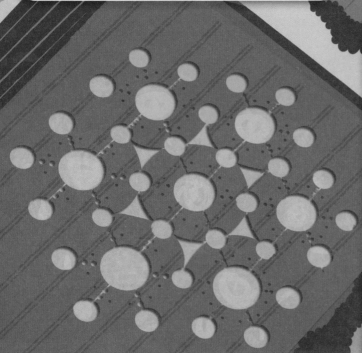

Crop circles may not be a recent phenomenon. There are stories from the sixteenth and seventeenth centuries about fairies and elves dancing in fields and leaving special circles in the grass. A picture dating from 1678 shows the 'Mowing Devil' making a circle in a field of oats.

In July 1880 a science journal called *Nature* published a letter from a scientist who had found several circular areas of flattened wheat on a farm in southern England. He suggested they were caused by 'some cyclonic wind action'.

Since the 1990s the patterns have become more complicated and include huge, intricate geometrical patterns. Whoever or whatever is making them is very good at maths as they are precisely designed and made.

Circles in the Ice

In North America, northern Europe and Russia people have spotted mysterious circles in frozen rivers and lakes. Some have been seen on ice that would be too thin for anyone to stand on to make the shapes.

Ice can naturally make circular patterns where water has been moving, but some of these circles have appeared in still water.

Intriguing Word

phenomenon

means something that you can see exists or happens, but you may not be able to explain why it exists or happens!

Turn over to read the **case file** notes...

CASE FILE - Crop Circles
The evidence so far...

Turn back to read the stories behind the case file...

Description

Circular swirling shapes or more complex designs including triangles and interlocking forms.

The average size for a crop circle is around 60-90 metres (200-300 feet) in diameter. The Milk Hill circle is extra large.

Time

Whoever or whatever is making them usually does it at night.

Location

Seen around the world, but mainly in the southern county of Wiltshire, UK.

Photographic Evidence

Many photos exist of these circles. No witnesses seem to have taken any film of them actually being made, except by people faking them!

They are all made by pranksters and hoaxers.

Chief Suspects

In September 1991 two British men, Doug Bower and Dave Chorley said they had made all the crop circles in England using a plank of wood, a ball of string and a wire eyepiece attached to a baseball cap! They admitted they had been inspired by the story of a crop circle discovered by a farmer in Australia.

These circles would be very complicated to make accurately overnight and in the dark. There are also just too many crop circles for them all to have been made by hoaxers.

Main Theories

Some witnesses say that these circles appear over invisible energy lines in the landscape called leylines. They believe that these leylines under the earth connect ancient sites like Stonehenge and the pyramids of Egypt.

They are landing sites for alien craft or messages from extraterrestrials.

They are caused by freaky weather. Small whirlwinds might make the circle patterns. However, could they really make such complicated designs?

UFO Suspects

In September 1974 a farmer from Saskatchewan in Canada reported seeing five small grey domes hovering over his crops. As they rose into the sky a blast of mist flattened the field into strange 'swirled' circles, leaving the rest of the field untouched. Other cases have also been reported. Some people have heard odd buzzing noises or even seen strange lights over fields where crop circles have then been discovered.

CEREOLOGY is the name given to the study of crop circles.

Further Investigation

Farmers may give you permission to visit their crop-circle fields.

Could the causes of ice circles be similar?

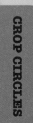

The Missing Lighthouse Men

In December 1900 a newly built lighthouse on a remote Scottish island was the scene of a mystery that has never been solved to this day.

On the night of 15th December an American ship was passing Eilean Mor, the biggest of the Flannan Isles. The captain noticed that there was no light coming from the lighthouse. He reported this, but bad weather from 17th December stopped anyone from sending a boat out to investigate until the 26th. Assistant lighthouse keeper Joseph Moore was on board the *Hesperus* as it approached Eilean Mor.

There was no reply to the ship's whistle and no one came to greet them at the landing platform. Moore ran up to the lighthouse and hammered on the door. Three lighthouse keepers should have been on duty, but there was no reply. Nervously, he opened the unlocked door and stepped inside. There was absolutely no sign of life inside the lighthouse: the clock had stopped; the beds were unmade; but the kitchen was neat and tidy. Most puzzling of all, the light seemed to be in perfect working order.

As Moore looked around he noticed that one set of oilskin waterproofs had been left hanging in the hallway. Where were the other two sets and where on earth were the three lighthouse men?

The crew of the Hesperus searched the island. On one of the landing platforms a box used for storing ropes had completely disappeared, leaving only a tangled mass of rope.

An enormous piece of rock had also been dislodged from the cliff above. But, lower down, a crane used for unloading boats was unharmed.

On 29th December Superintendent Robert Muirhead of the Northern Lighthouse Board arrived on Eilean Mor to conduct his own investigation. He was disturbed to read some odd entries in the lighthouse log.

The log entry for 12th December said that a huge storm with severe winds was raging around the island. Strangely, it also noted that one of the men, Donald McArthur had been crying.

The log for 13th December said the weather was still terrible and that the men were praying. This was odd because the bad weather had not started until 17th December.

The final log entry was on the morning of the 15th December. It stated:

'Storm ended, sea calm. God is over all.'

So what could have happened to the three lighthouse keepers of the Flannan Isles after this final log entry?

Turn over to read the **case file** notes...

CASE FILE - Flannan Isles Disappearances
The evidence so far...

Turn back to read the story behind the case file...

Location

The Flannan Isles are seven small, rugged islands off the coast of the Hebridean island of Lewis in Scotland.

TIMELINE OF EVENTS

15th December - no light from lighthouse reported by a passing ship.

17th-25th December - bad weather prevents anyone going to investigate.

26th December - Lighthouse Board boat Hesperus, makes it to the island. No sign of the three lighthouse men.

29th December - Superintendent Muirhead visits. Reads mysterious entries in log.

There was no radio or phone contact in those days.

The Victims

James Ducat, Principal Keeper

Thomas Marshall, Second Assistant

Donald McArthur, Occasional Keeper

Main Theory

Two of the lighthouse men went out to mend some storm damage. The third man observed a huge, freak wave coming towards them. He rushed out to warn them. All three were swept out to sea.

Clues

* Gate and doors neatly shut but left unlocked.
* Everything tidy indoors, and the light is primed for use.
* One of the three sets of oilskins is left indoors.
* Massive damage to some of landing stage area.
* Crane is undamaged.
* Lighthouse logbook contains weather reports and comment on McArthur being upset.

Beware - False Evidence!

Over the years the sad story has grabbed people's imagination. Poems, songs and even an opera have been written about the mystery. The strangest of theories have been dreamt up including the magical transformation of the men into massive black seabirds!

Many Unsolved Questions...

Why was the lighthouse door neatly shut? If there had been an emergency then surely the third man would not have had time to close it?

Why did the log mention McArthur crying? He was known to be a tough character.

Why did the weather reported in the log not match the weather elsewhere? The storms did not start until 17th December.

Was the landing stage damaged before or after 15th December?

Why were no bodies ever washed ashore?

FURTHER CASES TO INVESTIGATE

The *Mary Celeste* - a ship discovered drifting with no sign of its crew in 1872.

The vanishing soldiers - an entire battalion of British soldiers disappeared without trace in 1915 during a First World War battle at Gallipoli in Turkey.

The mystery of the Bermuda Triangle - an area of the Atlantic Ocean where planes and boats mysteriously disappear.

Mystery Word

inexplicable means something is impossible to explain.

MYSTERY WORDS EXPLAINED

Apparition means the strange and unexpected appearance of someone or something.

Archaeologist finds out about people who lived in the past by digging up ancient sites and studying the objects found there.

Cereology is the name given to the study of crop circles.

Coincidence is when two or more similar things happen at the same time, sometimes in an unlikely or freaky way.

Conspiracy means plotting with other people to do something bad or harmful.

Cryptozoology is the study of mysterious animals that may or may not exist.

Extrasensory Perception (ESP) is a special ability to predict what will happen in the future.

Extraterrestrial means coming from outside planet Earth. A being from outer space.

Geometrical means to be made up of shapes like circles, triangles and rectangles.

Illusion is something that is not really what it seems to be. Like a dream.

Incineration is when something is burnt to ashes.

Inexplicable describes something that is impossible to explain.

Leyline is an invisible energy line in the landscape believed by some people to connect ancient sites like Stonehenge and the Pyramids.

Megalith is a massive stone sometimes used as one standing stone or to build stone circles.

Neuroscientist studies the nervous system - the brain, the spinal cord and the nerve cells.

Objective means based on real facts, not on feelings and beliefs.

Paranormal means something that does not have an obvious scientific explanation.

Parapsychology is the study of mental abilities that cannot be explained by what scientists know about nature and the world.

Phantom is another word for ghost, apparition or spectre.

Phenomenon means something that you can see exists, but you may not be able to explain why it exists!

Phosphorescent is light that glows softly without producing heat, like a glow stick.

Premonition is a strong feeling that something unpleasant or horrible is about to happen.

Prophecy is a prediction about what will happen in the future.

Pseudoscience means theories that are NOT based on science.

Psychic means having special mental abilities like being able to read minds or tell the future.

Psychokinesis is the ability to move or bend objects using the power of the mind.

Psychometry is the ability to detect information about someone by touching objects belonging to them.

Rhabdomancy is another name for dowsing with rods, or water divining.

Spectre is another word for a ghost, phantom or apparition.

Spontaneous human combustion is when a person bursts into flames and the cause cannot be found.

Supernatural describes something that cannot be explained by what we know about the world around us.

Transformation is when something or someone changes into something else.

Uncanny means something is mysterious and difficult to explain.

UFO stands for Unidentified Flying Object. (It may or may not be an alien spaceship!)

Ufology is the study of unidentified flying objects (UFOs).

Undulating means moving like a wave, either up and down or side to side.